What to Do with These Red Flags?

UNLOCKING HEALTHY RELATIONSHIPS
FROM THE PENNANTS WITHIN

Martika Shanel

/INSPAREAD
Inspiring a read.
Lexington

Printed in the United States of America.

For permission or general information,
address Insparead,
insparead@insparead.com

www.insparead.com
www.martikashanel.com

Insparead books are published and distributed by Insparead.

ISBN 978-1-951101-11-4

Cover Design by Kiah Arnold

Edited by Kirsten McNeill
Production by Martika Shanel

First Edition: September 2021

Library of Congress 2021916131

contents

To Penelope, Hugh, and Wynn:
Look within for the love your heart desires.

preface

We must deep dive and look within ourselves when discussing the decision to pursue relationships we know aren't good for us. What is it about our personalities that causes us to choose unwisely? Why does this happen?

These questions led me to write the book--encouraging us to examine if we're looking within first for what we desire. Because dating when we have ourselves together is ideal. Are we centered? Do we know our likes and our dislikes? Do we really know ourselves?

It's a disservice when we jump into a relationship, then begin a quest of self-discovery. We have to admit, finding oneself after committing to someone is kind of backwards. Now, there's no way of getting it right 100% of the time, but the odds are more in your favor when going into a relationship where you and your partner fully understand each other apart from the union.

When this isn't done, either you grow together in a healthy way, or you grow apart because you've evolved into two people who no longer fit the relationship. The latter's the bigger pill to swallow and why some of us choose to stay.

Why *is* it so difficult to leave? Why is it that we really think a person is going to change when they've consistently revealed themselves to us? And why do we avoid seeing the flaws within ourselves? In a relationship where we're not getting the things that we need or we're allowing someone to take, why is it hard for us to choose the better pain? Why remain? The answer is simple when asked that way. But if anyone gets why it's easier said than done, it's me.

As a child, I was often overlooked; the one chosen last.
And I was conditioned to be a codependent, to accept the bare minimum when it came to acts of love. On my birthdays, for example, after the age of six, minimal effort was put into celebrating me.

Being on the receiving end of broken promises, I thought I wasn't worthy of nice things or true commitment. With the exception of my high school graduation, my celebratory moments were broken. Common phrases I heard were: "I started to do this for you." "I thought about doing this for you." "I wanted to do this for you, but…" This set the tone for how I received "love" in relationships.

As I got older, I was flattered if a person just thought of me. That was enough. We're all deserving of being celebrated and shown genuine appreciation; however, it wasn't shown to me to become an expectation of mine.

These interactions, during my formative years, culminated into the perfect recipe for me having minimal standards in relationships in general - friendships, associations, romances.

I really wanted people to not just like me but to love me. So at points, I internalized the longing for people to love me. I searched hard for that love and acceptance. It became the most important thing. Forget getting to know who I was and loving myself. No. Seeking outside acceptance was it. And I excelled at masking it, of course, so you couldn't tell by being around me there was an internal battle. But it existed.

It wasn't until my late 20s when I realized that if no one celebrated me, I would. I elevated to a place where no one had the authority over my peace and happiness; I'd given it back to myself. It's utter bliss having arrived here.

Before the revelation, there were several uncertainties in terms of who I was. I faced my red flags. I addressed them.

My hope is that this book helps you do the same.

SMITTEN

BEING SMITTEN AWAKENS ONE'S EAGERNESS TO FILL AND END THE DAY WITH LOVE, SO THEY MAY WAKE AND DO IT ALL OVER AGAIN FOR THE ONE WHO HOLDS THEIR HEART.

smitten

You're inseparable. People keep saying how much happier you are, how you're the perfect fit. And this may be true. But, I have to ask, how many red flags would you be holding if you showed your hand?

Yes. Everyone has flaws. I'm speaking to the things that make you cringe or furrows your brows. You know, *you* know:

- **How they treat others.** This is imperative to analyze and is a sound dealbreaker. Why so, you may ask? If a person is willing to speak to others without regard, withholds apologies for wrongdoings, or doesn't flinch when they upset someone, what makes you think you'll never be on the receiving end of this? Sidenote: Not all honeymoon phases last forever.
- **The family dynamics.** Remember, if this thing goes all the way, their family becomes your family. More importantly, there's chance that your partner will mirror the behavior you see from their parental figures. Are you okay with that?
- **Their relationship with money.** Do they spend it before they have it? Need a co-signer? Or are they too conservative with their money for your liking?
- **Their perceived future.** How do they envision their future? Or do they at all? Do their goals pass the SMART test (specific, measurable, attainable, relevant, and time-based)? What actions are they taking to breathe life into these goals?

These are simply a few. We shouldn't be cynical; however, we should analyze one's actions, especially when we're dating for marriage or long-term partnerships. Our aim is a healthy balance between the three lives in a relationship: yours, your partner's, and the union itself. This harmony is disrupted when we ignore the red flags, go through with an exclusive relationship, then examine the precautions in hindsight.

Have we not all been there? We take the long haul with a person, only to end up saying things like, "I saw the signs, but chose to ignore them" or "I should've seen this coming". It stinks when this happens. But how much heartache and time could we save if we'd just trust the process of connecting with *our* person?

Even though the experience may be fun with a person, and we find ourselves thinking of them at every turn, we owe it to ourselves to hop down from cloud nine, and look at the facts. Based on our calculations, is this person apt to leave when the fun runs out? Capable of being emotionally available for us when needed? Everyone's not clairvoyant, but that doesn't mean we shouldn't be realistic about what's in front of us.

Let's go back to the drawing board: the beginning--when everything is peachy keen. It's euphoric, right? It's as if you know they're the one. In fact, you question the idea of "where've they been all my life," "Is this my soulmate or twin flame?", which keeps racing through your mind. In essence, how *were* you living without them?

And that's how it starts.

Instead of comparing/contrasting how the two of you are incompatible and the potential long-term effects of this, you tell yourself that everything's perfect; it'll buff itself out.

And we all know how this story ends…

It's easier said than done, but what I can tell you, is when you love yourself more than a relationship, you can choose to exit and get on to a better you. And baby, the energy is more aligned when you do.

Upon exiting, reflect; do a deep, internal review to get to the root of it all. Yes. The "hindsight is 20/20" aspect. It's when the remnants of that euphoric dust connect with the surface of reality we realize how forced our efforts were. It's in following thoughts we grasp they were never our long-term person. It's unbelievable how we do that, huh?

We'll give a person years of our lives, our time, and our bodies only to realize that, at the inception of meeting them, our cut-off game should have been the strongest. In the ultimate beauty of these moments, we learn the biggest, eye-opening lessons we would not have otherwise.

...those catch-22 caveats…

Did your mind wander to all those what-ifs too? Here's the part where we dissect how to make more conscious choices. As clichéd as it sounds, it starts within.

Before entering romantic relations, there are important questions we should ask ourselves:

1) Am I entering this relationship to heal from a past one?
2) Is the purpose of this relationship to help me find myself?
3) Do I believe this relationship will help me feel less lonely or uplift me?

4) Am I making this relationship work because I believe this is the only person who will choose me?
5) Is my reason for choosing this relationship because I feel like time's ticking and I want to start a family?
6) Since I've never experienced love, is my decision based on that to see where this goes?

If you answered yes to any of these, your season is a journey of understanding who you are, not a romantic endeavor with someone. Now's the time to pour into you. It may be a scary thought - letting go of what you thought would be or could have been - however, embarking on this journey of self-discovery will be the best one you'll ever take. The one dedicated to uncovering your layers; truly knowing who you are and what self-care means to you.

UNDERSTANDING YOU

LIFE IS SAID TO BEGIN WITH A MYRIAD OF THINGS; IN ESSENCE, IT BEGINS WHEN YOU KNOW EXACTLY WHO YOU ARE TO THE CORE.

understanding you

Prior to being involved with someone, you've got to know who you are. For some of us, taking a period of time to befriend and shower ourselves with the love we envision is contrary to what we've seen and been encouraged to do. Knowing what your dealbreakers are, what you won't settle for, your preferences and values, et cetera, are essential. You must know what you want, so you're not making wavering appeasements in an attempt to maintain a relationship, and you can confidently stand erect in who you are.

exercise.

Let's make a list:

___/___/20___

_______________________'s List

(Insert Name)

Things I Love About Me

- ____________________
- ____________________
- ____________________
- ____________________
- ____________________

Growth Opportunities

- ____________________
- ____________________
- ____________________
- ____________________
- ____________________

Top Three Qualities I Desire in a Mate:

1. ____
2. ____
3. ____

Non-Negotiables

- ____________________
- ____________________
- ____________________
- ____________________
- ____________________
- ____________________

On top of knowing and honing these aspects, you should have airtight boundaries (this can be super hard, I know), and here's why: once you start moving the goalpost for your boundaries, the potential for chipping away at your being begins. Yes, we're human and we should give grace at our discretion; however, not when it's at your detriment or when it eats at the very fibers of who you are.

The most important factor in all of this is your vision. What does that look like for you? How do you envision yourself and your surroundings in the future, and does this person's outlook align with yours? Can the two of you build together? Is the support and encouragement mutual?

You may be thinking, my marriage or partnership is eternal; nonetheless, always remember that the only thing you can control is yourself.

We're not being cynical over here, just realistic. If we embrace this early on, life will flow more easily for us. Moreover, if we hold true to this, if the love for the relationship runs out, it will save us the heartache of trying to uncrumple a piece of paper, which will never happen.

RED FLAGS

You thought the red flags were a carnival, too, huh?

red flags

We've discussed a few red flags already. Let's dig deeper and ask ourselves:

Why do we choose to ignore common issues that end a relationship? Why is it, even when we know better, we don't do better? What's the real origin of this?

There's something within us that needs repairing when we stay on course with something long past its expiration date. And let's face it, when does forcing something ever work?

When you have a healthy foundation of self-love, you can make the tough decision to leave before it begins to change who you are for the worst. If you've been there, you know how an unhealthy tie to someone can bring out a not-so-nice version of the both of you.

At the beginning of nearly all relationships, there's this sense of "everything's perfect". It's what frames the relationship. If everyone's internal matters are unresolved, what starts to appear? One little red flag at a time. We convince ourselves that we can deal with them. It becomes our normal.

As time passes, it goes from being this perfect relationship into something with too much friction.

Then, a shift happens.

Everyone decides if they're going to stay and make the necessary repairs. However, if no one works on their red flags, how can anything get fixed?

When this is prolonged, we look back and realize we should've seen it coming. We may even find ourselves saying it's the other person who's in the wrong, making the relationship appear to be one perfect person and one problem person. That can't be.

The perceived perfect person is to blame too. Perhaps they didn't have boundaries, for example, so they gave too much. Or maybe they overextended themselves in a different capacity. It's possible that a person stayed knowing their mate wasn't in the right headspace for a relationship, wasn't interested in the long-term; or when they didn't have a primary foundation established, like employment, housing, transportation.

Despite seeing the wavering flags, the perceived perfect person goes on to make their partner the center of their universe, pouring into them even if there's little to no reciprocity.

At this point, the perceived perfect person should leave. But what do we know about them? They seldom leave when they should. It's a cycle: they give more in hopes of the love they want; they don't get it; they give more. The cycle may last for years.

You can't love someone into loving you.

When a person's actions don't match what you're looking for, which you've repeatedly expressed, it's time to exit. And that's the misstep. The perceived perfect person doesn't leave, initiating the blame game instead and the victimization starts.

This is when the journey of self-examination, an executive meeting with the self, should commence. Why in the world did it take years of a heavy heart and mounds of unfavorable situations for you to say, "you know what? Now I'm finally leaving"? That is a self-issue.

This issue has to be addressed, and it cannot be until accountability is taken. That's when the crash and burn happens, and you're subjected to your own metamorphosis, to sit with your, and your partner's ignored red flags.

You're forced to face them; understand what they are, how to rise above them. That is accountability. If you're wise, you'll work on them the first time around. We're human, so sometimes we have to get burned before we address what's going on from within.

When you understand why the unthinkable in your relationship had to happen, you're led to the holy grail.

INTERNAL REFLECTION

ACKNOWLEDGING AND ACTING ON THE RED FLAGS WITHIN YOURSELF AND OTHERS IS SELF-CARE; A BUILDING BLOCK OF SELF-LOVE.

internal reflection

Like many of us, my situation had everything to do with my upbringing and social interactions as a child. It wasn't until my mid-twenties when I learned that my behavior in relationships were based on a co-dependent attachment style, which I'd been programmed to foster as a child.

Coming up, I always knew my parents loved me. They encouraged the academia-first mindset and instilled in me that I could become whomever my heart desired. Furthermore, I understood the importance of commitment as I wasn't allowed to skip practice for sports teams I'd joined or not attend functions because I didn't feel like it.

These key principles helped propel me into my countless successes. What was the problem then?

Amid my parents acknowledging my achievements, supporting my extra-curricular involvements, and cheering me on from the sidelines, they struggled with addiction to prescription drugs (opioids), and, I'd later learn, to crack cocaine.

This presented a problem because despite their own successes, my mom earning a bachelor's degree and my dad serving a short stint in the military, we never had discretionary income, which led to various traumatic experiences I endured. I found myself taking on the parental role, having difficulties expressing my true feelings in all relationships, and valuing the approval of others more than my own. It even came to a point where I wondered why I existed.

I'd give money to my parents up until my first big-girl job in corporate America. When I analyzed my interactions with other relationships, I would over give, and overextend myself as a way of showing my love because that's what I thought defined love. I'd do this in hopes of getting love in return. And when I look back, it was an unhealthy dependence on relationships.

I had also developed an exaggerated sense of responsibility for others' actions because that's what I'd been groomed to do as a child.

What did this look like? Plain and simple: hyper empathy. So, if you had a problem and we discussed it, as the conversation came to an end, it became our problem. And I'd move mountains, pushing my needs and goals aside to help equip you with the tools and resources needed for your success. I made it my mission to fix others' problems.

I would insert myself in someone else's predicament to help them. Meanwhile, I had issues of my own that I never stopped to analyze. I didn't pour into myself as I was pouring into others. You're the most important person in your life, and you're supposed to pour into yourself first. I wasn't taught that. And I didn't fully understand that concept and apply it until embarking on my 30th birthday.

Now, don't get me wrong, helping others is a great thing, and I pride myself on doing so when it's feasible. Before I learned these lessons, my help for others meant I sacrificed time and money I didn't have. It got to a point where I would silence my inner voice and feelings when it didn't sit well with me because "they needed my help", and "I had to be the one to do it, right?".

As you can see, this view on love is an unhealthy one. No relationship should be built upon what you can do for others in hopes of affection in return. That's not how love works.

The love I was seeking, that we should all seek, is internal love. This is one of the aspects of empowerment and enabling yourself to exit a relationship when it's no longer working for you, and allowing others to leave when they have the same realization.

We have to get to a point where our ultimate goal is unconditional happiness. Once we have that, no one has ownership of our feelings. It may be confusing when we say, "someone made me feel this way" because we control our own emotions. And when we don't, we're dependent on other people to bring us this source of happiness, or validation. In the same breath, we give them governance over us, allowing the same people to bring us misery instead of knowing we have a choice.

We always have a choice to remove ourselves from situations to assess what's going on internally, to understand why we're allowing things we don't appreciate to occur. Why didn't we put our foot down? Where's our backbone?

This should lead us to the point where we love ourselves enough to find our happiness. When we're at peace with being alone, there's a feeling of pure bliss because that's something external sources or people can't bring to us.

Part of getting to a blissful state is assessing past hurt. Whether it's from childhood trauma, a traumatic relationship, or any devastating experience, we have to address it. This doesn't mean you have to get over what happened to you, but to face it, so you may live and function through it.

We're further aligned with our purpose when we face our pain and elevate beyond it. An imperative component is having inner peace. Just like unconditional happiness, if we're lacking inner peace, then we're looking to everyone and everything around us to fulfill the need, which is unhealthy. A relationship is meant to satisfy both people from a healthy standpoint.

As we move closer to internal tranquility, it's not up to our loved ones to facilitate our therapy sessions. They're not in a qualified position. Sometimes, professional help is warranted when we're combating childhood trauma and other emotional wounds.

You may think you're operating just fine, but if your relationships are rocky or you're seeing a common denominator amongst them, it may be you who needs healing. We owe it to ourselves to be balanced and that requires us to have inner synergy.

If one aspect of our mental state is skewed it will affect how we operate. Take our emotions, for example. If we're on edge, reacting to conflicts versus responding to them, we create chaos and instability for ourselves and those around us. If we're internalizing everything and automatically put ourselves in an unpleasant mindset, this habit needs to be addressed.

It's up to us to hold ourselves accountable for identifying the issue and understanding that we can't continue on such a path and still function in a normal capacity. When I deliberated on my feelings toward certain situations, I accepted that I had unresolved issues. I noticed that I got upset when someone didn't show up the way I thought they should've. My reaction was to internalize the situation and allow that to negatively affect my emotions when I'm the one responsible for them.

No one can make me feel a certain way. I finally understood that if I had boundaries and showed up for myself how I wanted others to, the energy and reciprocity I longed for would come. If we have our non-negotiables in place and enforce them, a person can't have dominance over our feelings.

It starts by assessing yourself at every level. Gauging your level of self-esteem and what you project into the universe. Do you have a positive perspective or does pessimism come naturally to you?

Liberation comes from confronting yourself. Personal issues must be addressed. True freedom and happiness appears when you know the essence of your inner self, and you're happy in your skin and can enjoy your company. There's no need to latch onto people or objects to bring you that. Holding yourself accountable and seeking to understand instead of being right is full liberation.

Saying, "I'm fine. I'll get through this on my own" is not enough. Whenever we're talking about situations that have hurt us, we have to heal. If not, we'll always find ourselves in broken relationships. We'll find ourselves playing the victim. It simply cannot be that you were Perfect Patty or Paul in a relationship with the other person doing all the damage, putting you through uncomfortable situations and making you feel a certain way. Let's put down the victim hat and be the victor of our own doings.

Once this hit home for me as a young adult, I knew I had to work to fix it. I had to detoxify my life. It didn't happen overnight. Not knowing how to healthily address it, i.e. internalizing hidden emotions and being passive aggressive, caused several rifts in my relationships that I had to work to repair.

Why am I sharing this? Had I taken the time to get to know who I was at the core, I could have identified my own red flags and avoided those difficult lessons.

It's safe to say we're never going to be perfect and get it right 100% of the time. But knowing ourselves will give us a better approach to how we foster present relationships and develop new ones.

exercise.

Let's take a dive into a past or current conflict we've had with a friend/loved one:

What happened?

____
____
____
____
____
____
____
____

What was the root cause?

____
____
____
____
____
____

Since we can only control ourselves, what could we have done differently that could've appeased the situation? Or negated it all together?

Life is more seamless once you embrace that you can only control yourself, your life, and your emotions.

I'll share two experiences as examples:

During the publication stage of my debut children's book "I Will Live My Best Life Too", I wore numerous hats getting the perfect book published, and one evening an avoidable situation occurred.

It was a little past ten when I couldn't get a particular technique down in Adobe Illustrator, despite watching several tutorials. To meet the publication deadline, I had to complete this for print.

This led me to asking someone with more experience for help: my then husband. Even though it was late, and he was playing his game, I expected him to help me anyhow.

He begrudgingly helped, and the situation ended on a sour note.

How could this have been avoided? I should've respected his me-time and tabled the task. Or better yet, I could've hired someone else earlier that day to complete the job. Both were things I could've controlled.

Five years prior, when I first moved to Chicago, another avoidable situation happened--

One of my closest friends, my boyfriend, and I agreed to rent an apartment together since we'd be working in the same city. She could not move in at the same time, so I agreed to pay her share until she could. A few months after moving in, she had to relocate. One of her suggestions was having a roomie take her place, which I didn't want but never voiced that or thought about beforehand.

Since she was leaving early, I felt she should pay me for the months I covered her share although we never discussed how we'd navigate a change in the agreement. It ended with me having bouts of anxiety during that period, and a breakdown at lunch with my manager after a meeting with a potential client. I remember the emotion building up to the point where I excused myself from our meal, raced to the restroom, and called a confidant, sobbing uncontrollably. The close friend and I didn't talk for a while.

How could this have been avoided? I shouldn't have given so much and thought about future scenarios, i.e. would I be comfortable living with someone I didn't know if it ever came to that? Had I considered these two items alone, the scenario would not have occurred. But it did because I was a yes person and an over-giver, who didn't know my boundaries, viewed giving as love, and had difficulty expressing my feelings. (Whew...the anxiety.)

As you see, I had a few red flags from both situations:

- Expecting others to assist me despite what they are doing because I did the same for them in previous situations

- Agreeing to a situation without analyzing every aspect and my preferences towards potential outcomes

- Investing more than I had to contribute by using money I needed for other expenses to cover the cost

The overall issue was not having boundaries and being reactionary when others did not respond how I felt they should've based on how I showed up for them.

exercise.

Let's continue to reflect on your conflict. Based on the details and your contributions, or lack thereof, what were/are your own red flags?

________________ ________________ ________________

________________ ________________ ________________

As we worked through this chapter, we've gained an understanding of the importance of reflecting internally, and why drawing the line on our non-negotiables and enforcing our boundaries are necessary to avoid tension. If friction arises, we can focus on the variables we can control.

“MIS”JUDGEMENT

“LOVE IS A FIRE.
BUT WHETHER IT
IS GOING TO
WARM YOUR
HEART OR BURN
DOWN YOUR
HOUSE, YOU CAN
NEVER TELL.”

JOAN CRAWFORD

“mis”judgement

Powerful statement by Joan.

But can’t we tell? Is it ever really missed? Did we misjudge the person we chose, or did we miss the judgement because we wanted the relationship to work. More than likely, it’s the latter. If we look back, chances are, there were several red flags that we decided to collect and tuck away.

We knew how they would treat us by the way they treated the waiter, spoke to their family, angrily reacted because they didn’t get their way. You see, we had a front row seat to hindsight viewing. There was a foreshadow to how they would emotionally impact our mental state from their expressed views on certain situations, and their banter on controversial topics. The bottom line is we deliberately decided to stay and force something that wasn’t meant to be.

When I look back, there were several instances that preluded what would happen in my first marriage. Although we had a grasp on who we were, we didn’t know ourselves to the core; had unresolved, childhood trauma; and our views on how to have a thriving union differed in crucial areas, like finances and honoring each other’s peace havens.

We went from being the best of friends and madly in love to allowing our differences to overshadow the bigger picture.

In the end: “You want to see what you want to see. You’re going to do what you want to do.” - My Granny, Connie Sue Barnes

FIGHT, FLIGHT, FREEZE, OR FAWN

HOW WE
RESPOND TO
CIRCUMSTANCES
DETERMINES OUR
PROXIMITY TO
OUR DESTINY.

fight, flight, freeze, or fawn

If only they could see me one last time. Me and all my glory. I mean, I'm an excellent catch; with a majority of the attributes a mate says they want. They must know they're going to miss me when I'm gone.

This isn't the case. This will never be the case.

You may have heard, many times over, that if a person loves you, they wouldn't leave you. And that's partly true. Maybe they do love you, but are leaving for themselves, or they've found another person who they feel is more capable of fulfilling their needs. Either way, there's nothing you can say or do to force their hand--to get them to "see" you: they already have. And the harsh truth is, you're not their person. They don't want to be with you.

The pain can cut even deeper if the person didn't wholeheartedly fight for the union. You are not their person if they're unwilling to exhaust every option to make it work.

Love is easy, not forced, so if you find yourself trying to make it work when there's an inkling of uncertainty that's out of your control, the door's always an option.

Because all relationships don't pan out how we envision, we must plan for how we'll successfully leave if we have to. Let's face it, people change with life experiences, and in the same breath, people have the freewill to change their minds about a relationship at any time, so let's talk exit strategy (psst...you should always have one.)

Think: what would I need to make a semi-seamless transition if my partner or I decided to leave the relationship (i.e. finances)?

Love's a gamble, and it's imperative that we consider this. Because if the relationship doesn't work, how will you regain stability?

This can be difficult to face; however, it'll be harder to get through or out of it if you're unwilling to accept the season your mate is in.

We mustn't forget that everyone's on their own journey, and sometimes it doesn't include you.

When you find yourself prying, pulling, and pressing to make it work, apply that pressure to your personal goals so you can grow. Because your actions are what you control. And why wouldn't we want to witness our own wins?

Fight. Should you fight for your relationship? Absolutely. You should work to repair it if y'all are both willing to put forth the effort, enhancing who you are individually so you can improve collectively. And what I can also reassure you of is that you'll need to choose the flight option if there's only one dog in the fight.

Flight. There's no need sticking around when the other person's actions/inactions or your own are screaming, "Where's the exit?!"

The quicker you pass "go", the quicker you start the healing process and getting through the five stages of grieving--denial, anger, bargaining, depression, and acceptance. But, let's be real. How many of us are grounded enough to use the door when we realize it's not working?

(Pssst...we're getting there.)

Freeze and fawn. For those in this bracket, what do we do? We freeze and fawn, thinking “I might as well stay because I don’t believe the odds are favorable if I fight or flee”, becoming numb. Or we’ll make it our mission to try and win over their heart regardless of our true feelings, which is often at the expense of our emotions, sensations, and needs--fawning.

When we find ourselves in a predicament where we’ve succumbed to the latter two options, we’re in a dire need of a heart-to-heart with ourselves.

THE EFFECTS OF IGNORING RED FLAGS

A GREATER INVESTMENT DOESN'T ALWAYS EQUATE TO THE REWARD FOR WHICH WE HOPED.

the effects of ignoring red flags

What happens when we choose to go along despite the telltale evidence that states this isn't a good fit? How does this all pan out?

From my experience, I can tell you verbatim the outcome that looms. For starters, the romance will be great. In fact, you'll even go to great lengths to make sure of it. Next, comes the resurfacing of your red flags and theirs; this will be cancerous to the relationship, and once it's full blown, in will sail the "I should haves".

Just like any malignant cancer, the earlier it's detected and diagnosed, the greater chances of a cure. But in relationships, the likelihood of curability lessens when there's denial, stubbornness, and outright selfishness.

If we acknowledge these improvement areas within ourselves, we can start the betterment project for personal growth. And as we're working on ourselves from the inside out, our partner should also make a conscious initiative to do the same.

It can't be that one partner's on the self-improvement path, and the other's not. There has to be a concerted effort to enhance each other, to improve the relationship.

Let's face it, as we move through life, our preferences change and our outlook shifts. That's normal. The flip side is working to keep the relationships we value intact, which requires dedication.

Bottom line: when we collect our partner's red flags in the smitten stage, they'll later mesh with our own; and when left unaddressed, the two of you will begin to resent one another. You'll build a wall so high that neither of you can see over it to rekindle the flame that once withstood the gustiest of winds. Eventually, the wall will divide you in such a manner, that one thing is bound to happen:

The two of you will mentally and emotionally leave the relationship, and one partner will emotionally and physically move on with someone else.

SELF-LOVE

GIVING THE BEST
OF YOURSELF
TO THE
UNDESERVING
RAISES THE
QUESTION,
WHERE'S THE
SELF-LOVE?

self-love

I always operated by the rule of no one owes me anything. But I found myself doing things by "rule of thumb" - honoring people a certain way because of a title - without applying the idea that I don't owe anyone anything either. I would love from a place of perceived guilt and obligation. And instead of sewing the love I wanted into myself, I did the opposite: reserving the way I wanted to be loved for everyone but me.

My self-love meter was so low that if someone disrespected me in any way, I wouldn't allow the opportunity to defend myself. When later left alone with my thoughts, I'd internalize the situation and self-ridicule because I didn't take an appropriate stance, making light of the situation instead.

I was an emotional wreck, mashing deep-rooted pain with disingenuous happiness. This changed once I got a better grasp of who I was, and looked at the root of why I tolerated this.

The bottom line was I needed help in the self-respect department and that was tied to how much I loved myself.

In relationships, it's imperative that respect is somewhere on our list of non-negotiables.

If I had only applied this to prior relationships, I would've saved myself a multitude of hurt. The truth is, once the line of disrespect is crossed, and only half-baked apologies are given, expect this cycle to continue. The disrespect will reappear in different facets and the hurt will thicken. At this point, you're in a cycle of insanity expecting a different effect.

Be mindful that your value is intrinsic—no one can giveth and no one can taketh away.

We have to choose ourselves. At the end of the day, your happiness and your peace mean so much more than keeping any relationship together. When it starts to erode your sanity, and your mental and emotional well-being, you have to take charge and understand that is unhealthy. And if your partner has expressed to you that hey, they're unwilling to meet you halfway for an intervention, such as counseling, your best bet is to move on.

That's not your person. Someone who's unwilling to make the relationship work is not your destined mate. It's going to be hurtful; it's going to be painful. I've been there, and the raw truth is: you can't force a genuine relationship on someone else. Focus on what you can control.

Waiting hopelessly for a person to change is not the most viable option. And waiting for them to change without working on you isn't going to cut it either. Once you leave to rebuild, start working on yourself from the inside out. That's when the real work begins. You will get closer to your destiny and your purpose, to your future achievements, to that state of balance that you've been seeking. But waiting around for someone to pick you is going to delay this process.

And if a person chose you at the beginning, are they still choosing you? That's the real question. Do you still matter that much to them that they're willing to put in more effort to make it work? Because if you're answering no or *maybe* to that, then maybe they're not your person.

And that's okay. Everyone can't remain with you as the seasons continue to change and vice versa.

And I get it. We want to be loved, to be chosen by someone who matches our steez; however, have you considered that regardless of if you're tied to another person, you already possess the qualities of a spouse? You don't happen to be a wife or a husband, and that's okay.

We are worthy whether or not we are connected to someone else. I know the societal pressure of being in a committed relationship exists and how not having a mate or being a single/co-parent may appear to others. But what outweighs that is getting to a point where we're so comfortable and so confident in our current situation because we've attained unconditional happiness and internal peace, that it doesn't matter what society thinks. It's better to be in a state of tranquility and serenity, than to be in an undesirable relationship.

It's all about reframing our minds to understand that it's okay that things didn't work out. It's when we start to force relationships that they become damaging to what we have going on in our lives.

Think about it in terms of your wardrobe. Would you wear a pair of jeans that were too tight? Bearing unnecessary discomfort throughout the day when you could simply put on a pair more suitable for your frame? That's the point we've gotten to in society. It tells us that "hey, just wear the jeans. I know it's uncomfortable, but wear them." We have to change the narrative, no longer remaining in relationships that create distance between us and where we're supposed to be; who we're supposed to become; what we're supposed to achieve. All because we've chosen to put unnecessary pressure on a union that's no longer sustainable.

Let's move past the need to put on a facade for everyone. Yes, you should honor your commitment, but not to the extent that the appearance everyone sees is a complete 180 from what's going on at home. And I'm not talking about the one-offs where you have a disagreement or a terrible argument. I'm not talking about the conflicts that leave a constant temperature in the room where everyone being unhappy is the norm.

The pets are unhappy. The children are unhappy. It's a contagious energy that doesn't have to be. That's what we have to acknowledge.

Before my ex-husband and I exchanged vows, we discussed how we'd never stay together for the children or use that as a crutch. Granted, our ending wasn't seamless, to say the least, but the conversation was made.

Now we're in a positive co-parentship, and our children have two happy homes. Yes, everything's nice, everything's beautiful when you tie the knot, but we mustn't forget the difficult conversations beforehand. Of course, you think it's going to last forever. Who doesn't? Who gets married to say, "you know what, I'm gonna put in two years and then give my resignation"? Who invests all their time, energy, and finances into something they know won't give them the ROI they're seeking?

Life happens. Our circumstances change. External issues happen during the course of the relationship--jobs, location, finances, and family matters. Additionally, there are the internal matters that go on within you and your partner. Each of you are evolving into who you're supposed to be. So as the two of you are changing, your alignment with each other is going to as well. It's inevitable. And if both people are unwilling to say, "although I'm changing and so are the things around us, I'm still gonna fight for this and give an extra 10% to preserve what we have", the relationship is over.

If we truly comprehend that, whenever we're confronted with this scenario, we'll understand that we may have to be the one who uses the door.

If we choose to stay when we know it's not working, something so crazy and so left field will happen that'll thrust you out of the relationship anyhow, because it's no longer a good fit.

Instead of asking if a person is right for you, here are the questions you have to ask yourself:

Are you the right person for yourself?

Are you undeniably in love with you?

PICK PEOPLE, NOT PROJECTS

BECAUSE WHEN HAS DATING POTENTIAL EVER WORKED?

pick people, not projects

A person can only be who they've presented themselves to be; ergo, it really is, "what you see, is what you get." If you're wanting a different version of that person, it's best for you to allow them to evolve without you. Because when we don't do this, we're vowing to accept a person who we've envisioned. That's not them. And we mustn't forget: unless they want to be that person, you will never see them.

Possessing the Savior Complex will get you to a certain point in relationships, so until you meet the person who mirrors your drive and outlook, invest in yourself; save yourself. Avoid using your time, energy, and resources building someone else's empire. That's their responsibility. Believe it or not, when this is done, it's not surprising when they choose to leave once they've reached their point of success, which brings me to my next point.

If you're solely committed to the relationship, expect your partner to bounce when they see fit. If you're feeling single in your relationship, I'm speaking to you. It's possible that you may be thinking "*maybe they need time to figure out that I'm really worth it; maybe they're confused about where they're at in life; maybe us taking a break will really do us some good."*

These may be valid points; nevertheless, how long will you reserve time (during your best years, might I add) for an indecisive person? For this person to decide that you're the prize, that you're a great person for their life?

Or what if they never return and you've invested over a decade of your life waiting for them to see you? Talk about resentment, eh? But this doesn't have to be the case. Your story can be how you've envisioned it, meeting the person who will be who they've professed to you. There will be no second guesses; not a shadow of a doubt about their feelings for you.

In fact, this person will outline their plans, and you will see them executing them. Their plans will include you and there will be no confusion in your spirit. Most importantly, the trust will be there. They're ready to proclaim their love for you from the mountain tops.

Take it from me, who sounded like a broken record for years on how I wanted to be loved. If a person is demonstrating that you're not the absolute apple of their eye, that you're not their person, it's imperative that you acknowledge that when first observed and, you guessed it, leave. Because there's nothing more painful than to keep investing in an emotional tie, only to feel used and abandoned when they've moved on (always remember the door's an option).

If you wouldn't keep putting your money in a vending machine after it's taken your coins, why would you keep pouring your time and energy into a relationship that isn't reciprocating what you're giving? You deserve someone who's going to love you the way that you want to be loved.

LISTEN TO YOUR SPIRIT

THAT UNEASY FEELING IS THERE FOR A REASON--LOOK INTO IT.

listen to your spirit

Your gut is your truth. I'm speaking to solely your gut, not the ideas that are imagined, but that nagging feeling that keeps drawing your attention. When that happens, you listen. Something's there. And more than likely, it's confirmation of everything you've been thinking.

Like several others, 2020 was a revealing year for me. Not only was I forced to face that my marriage was on fire, I had to marinate in the truths of relationships I had once cherished.

It seemed as if my world was ending, but in reality, it was the impetus of my evolution. During the post-partum depression and the depression from a heavy break up, I understood the layers that make up one's purpose.

Despite being an uber private person, I embraced the idea of being more transparent.

Listening to my spirit also placed me in a position to confront undertones that I subconsciously knew rested at bay. Had I not answered that little voice, that racing feeling in my chest, I'd still be steps from where I'm at now.

LIBERATION

INNER PEACE = LIBERATION

liberation

Want to free yourself? Achieve unconditional happiness and be genuinely content with your life? Getting there requires us to refocus our perspective. And we can start by changing our view on relationships.

As we meet new people and further develop the bonds we have with others, we must perceive these relations as unbound ties. Meaning, we have to remove expectations from others—doing things for them altruistically with no strings attached. Not only is this freeing, it's healthy. Furthermore, it can force us to examine the fruitfulness of our relationships and boundaries.

Once that happens, you can attract the energy your heart desires because there's no looming cloud of "someone owes me something."

Trust the process.

The person your heart yearns for is coming.

And while you await that alignment, go work on you. We all have areas of improvement to enhance. The best time to do this is during your selfish season. So if you're single, now's your time to shine alone (yasss).

If not, when you're desensitized, you create more distance between you and your destiny.

At the end of the day, inner peace is everything. And nothing should interfere with it. Protect it at all costs. Everything must be balanced in order for us to be centered mentally, physically, financially, spiritually, et cetera.

You have to save yourself. You have to come to terms with what season you're at in your life and fully commit to it. So, if it's your selfish season, let it be just that--taking the time to figure yourself out. You'll know when you're on the brink of your next season because you'll feel complete. You'll stand erect in who you are, and to top it off, everyone around you will see it. It's a beautiful feeling to be one with yourself wholeheartedly. I'm rooting for you!

How do you save yourself?

- Self-reflect.
- Understand your vision.
- Dive into how you will improve yourself for you.
- Place your time and energy into building and molding your craft.

exercise.

Let's see how this looks:

It's no secret that we shine differently when we're centered. Everything's in balance. Part of getting there is by noting your personal goals and slaying them.

Make a list of your personal goals, big and small. What do you want to accomplish some day?

__________________ __________________ __________________

__________________ __________________ __________________

__________________ __________________ __________________

Circle the ones that you can reach in the next 3-6 months.

Now, write out your declaration below for the one you wish to slay first and put a date on it:

I will ____

____by ___/___/20___.

The only thing left to do is map out our game plan! All that consists of, is defining a starting point and breaking down this goal piece-by-piece. We may not have the capacity to tackle everything at once, but we can little by little (this is my motto for everything, by the way, “poco a poco”).

Ask yourself:

What’s the first thing I need to get jump started, e.g. research, seek a mentor?

What resources do I already have or what's free to get started ASAP?

Lastly, mark your calendar, say your goal aloud, elicit help, get an accountability partner, and complete step one. Just like that, you're en route to conquering at least one goal within the year.

Even if your schedule's airtight, doing one big or small thing each day will get you there.

May the slayage begin.

IT'S THE SELF-CARE FOR ME

SHOWING YOURSELF THE CARE AND ATTENTION YOU DESERVE IS ESSENTIAL TO YOUR WELL-BEING, IT HONES YOUR INNER PEACE.

it's the self-care for me

You can't give what you don't have and that speaks to peace too. If you're entering a relationship with unhealed wounds and unresolved pain, it's difficult to be your mate's peace. You may get away with it for a while, but bet on the issue resurfacing when that issue's triggered.

Healing is the best self-care you can do for yourself. You can mask hurt and deep-rooted emotional discomfort for so long. Yes, the distractions feel good—the shopping, the social events, the relationships—but when are you going to address the internal conflicts that reappear when you're alone with your thoughts?

While awaiting the divorce to be final, I took a plunge into self-care. And let me tell you, it made all the difference. From the conversations with trusted ears, to getting back in the gym, to elevating and dating myself. I could go on and on.

It's been eye-opening getting to know myself for the first time.

What's crazy is looking back at how I neglected my self-care by being so involved with everyone else and understanding how that negatively affected my well-being.

Knowing what self-care measures work for you is essential. Here are some ideas I've incorporated:

physical

- consuming proper nutrients
- connecting with nature
- getting adequate rest
- exercising weekly

emotional

- speaking positively to yourself
- being kind to yourself
- setting and enforcing boundaries
- saying no as a complete sentence
- taking time before answering favors

social

- networking - personal/professional
- trying new venues
- removing unpleasant people
- showing up to support others

psychological

- showing gratitude
- reading/journaling
- taking a tech break
- learning a new skill

professional

- giving realistic deadlines
- setting clear boundaries
- requiring mutual respect
- taking breaks less interruption
- building your work portfolio

environmental

- organizing your space
- tidying up routinely
- giving back to the community
- reducing, reusing, recycling

exercise.

Self-Care Methods - How do you create your peace? What does that look like to you?

_______________ _______________

_______________ _______________

_______________ _______________

MAKING IT WORK

THE RECIPE FOR A SUCCESSFUL RELATIONSHIP: ALL PARTIES PUTTING IN WHAT THEY WANT FROM IT; SPEAKING EACH OTHER'S LOVE LANGUAGE WHILE EQUALLY POURING INTO THEMSELVES.

making it work

There are several theories on what makes a prosperous relationship, so how do we know which one works?

After taking a dive into my failed marriage and analyzing the glue that holds together the successful relationships around me, I'm confident in saying that I'm on to something.

Earlier, we introduced the importance of a healthy balance between the lives in a relationship: yours, your partner's, and the union itself, which I'll refer to as "the trio." The trio will thrive and have longevity if it has a healthy dose of reciprocation of whatever the two of you need to feel loved and accepted.

Remember: just being in a relationship doesn't signify that you're in love. These are some tips I've learned along the way:

- **Choose your words wisely.** You can never retract them.
- **Be mindful of your actions and inactions.** You cannot rewind time to re-do them.
- **Respond v. React.** Iterating the first two points, be careful with how you address situations and how you show up for people.
- **Be solution oriented.** When there's a problem, it best serves us to focus on the solution, not the issue.
- **Give the best version of yourself.** Your partner deserves your best and vice versa. Aim for mutual dignity, utmost respect, and love per respective love language.

- **Understand what your partner isn't.** Your partner's not your therapist or punching bag. If you're facing deep-rooted issues, seek professional help at your discretion.
- **Create space.** If you're enhancing your management of conflicts, choose space when things go awry to allow for a healthy response.
- **Have a healthy mindset.** Avoid racing to hypotheticals or immediately thinking the worst in situations.
- **Practice self-love and -care.** Treat and love yourself the way you wish to be treated and loved. Ensure you're taking care of yourself first, so you're in a healthy place to support your partner in the manner needed. Understand that your value is intrinsic. No one can deem its worthiness but you.
- **Do not settle.** If you're not getting what you want, voice it respectfully. If it isn't fulfilled given ample time, and you're meeting your partner's needs, it's time for an executive meeting with yourself. Is this what you want? If not, you'll want to consider your relationship because your peace is everything, and if you're repeatedly asking the same thing of someone, and it's left undone, perpetuating insanity will disrupt your joy.
- **Measure how much you care.** We should be our partner's main cheerleader, but sometimes, we can excessively care. And it can get to a level where we're seen as overbearing by our partner. This can lead to resistance, and if we're not careful, resentment. Because there's a healthy balance to this. When we overstep our boundary in this arena, we're really pushing them away.

Liken it to a job where you and your coworker are equals, but they insist on acting as your boss. If this has ever happened to you, you know exactly how you felt and how you wanted to avoid that person at every turn.

It's the same with children who feel smothered by their parents a majority of the time, which may lead them to intentionally creating distance between themselves and their parent(s).

In essence, care at their discretion not yours.

A relationship is a partnership where all parties are on the same playing field. Everyone plays for the same team and works on self-development to better the team. It's void of competition, aspiring to outshine the other. It's a commitment to work jointly to get the team as far ahead as possible.

Everyone has to be all in, but sometimes we can't be, which leads to an imbalance. That is how the relationship strengthens and grows. It's what helps to mold it because you lean on each other.

No one is ever 100% at all times. There will be times with deficiencies. And that's when your person steps in to uplift you, to make up for that imbalance. This can become unhealthy.

The uplifting becomes an issue when you're constantly picking up the slack from the other person. The person can't seem to get it together in any avenue, so if the support is from an emotional standpoint, you feel like you're putting all the emotion into the relationship. If it's a financial standpoint, you find yourself pulling from all your monetary resources when that isn't what was agreed upon. Granted, whatever you and your partner's recipe for success is, that's fine. It's whenever there's a consistent and almost permanent deviation from that when it's unhealthy, causing a rift in your relationship. Whether or not you can bounce back is on both parties.

Balance is key. There will be periods of darkness in the relationship, and one has to bring light for the other person. When both of you have that light, even better. It becomes problematic when there's darkness from both partners, and no one's willing to shine their light. Drag this out for too long and you see the relationship to its end.

How exactly does a couple keep the light flickering? Everyone has to deliberately choose peace and happiness. Both making the conscious choice to wake up on the right side of the bed. Deciding to act with good intentions and be in high spirits. And if something's blocking this, opting for professional help when warranted, because darkness becomes our focal point when we get ourselves in a negative headspace, dimming the flame.

Are you willing to build a barrier around your flame so that nothing can compromise it?

We must have those painful, yet necessary conversations. I think we can all agree they're not happy, go-lucky ones, but they're needed to preserve honesty. Being candid also includes how you feel about the two of you. How you feel about the partnership; whether or not it's working for you; how it's making you feel. And if you all want to repair it, how that'd look.

It's about those imperative discussions. Because if you both love each other, you will have that understanding, and if one person's feeling a way, maybe the other person does too and doesn't know how to say it.

Bottom line: have the conversation even if it's painful. Because to simply understand that something's not working and to move on without transparency is unfair to the other person. It can be avoided and should be taken seriously.

Mirror check. We have to face ourselves in relationships. There has to be accountability. Self-reflection is critical, and we must confront internal discord. This goes for all relationship types.

Healthily co-existing with your partner should be ideal. So if we're easily agitated and unable to contain our emotions, we need to understand why.

The fundamental key in all relationships is to work with others in a copacetic manner. Address it now or you'll have to later down the road.

POETIC EXCERPTS: TO MYSELF WITH LOVE

Ode to Self-Love

Beaming with glee, affirming one's self
The uncertainty of ego, imagined constraints
Shifted perspective, through an inner lens,
My truth commences.

New aura, who dis? Whose chin rises high
A glint of triumph in my eyes.
Who's bearing boldness and élan
Others' opinions, never a thought.

'Tis the confidence for me.
At ease with whom I'm intended to be
Self-aware and freed
The advice of Pindar, I heed

Yas! What comfort resides,
Laying in thine own mind.
Past actions, bleak,
Unraveling views, your validation I seek.

Dimming my light, obsolete
Unlearned, choices shading my view;
Making room for me, unapologetically--
This kind of love, not befriending the blues.

Shine

As you find your space,
rise above the odds, you'll do;
shine and take the leap.

Self-Love

Searching for acceptance, affirmation, and love
Eventual erosion of boundaries and esteem
Loveless moments woven 'tween the fabric of her being
Forever chasing a love complementary to her soul
Lucid love, effortlessly exchanged
Overt love, proudly displayed
Vast love, stemming from within
Extolling her beauty and self-worth first.

The search over, before it begins.

Prudent

Thought I'd met my forever companion
Like hell, I fought for that man
Him before me
His desires, the first I'd see
I'll be damned if I ever do that again

Hopeless Romantic

Hopelessly in love,
This time snubbed:
If not for this ill happenstance,
Would she e'er know true romance?

As the dust settles on this disunion,
Her person awaits--hallelujah!

I Choose Me

Standing at the mirror, I gaze at myself,
the thought arises full stop:
Maybe this *is* something I deserve?
Perhaps, if I'd done what was in my heart before,
I wouldn't have to ponder if we're in this happily,
questioning our love.

But then again, don't I owe it to myself,
to be in a romance, in love, happily?
To wonder if there is someone more whom I deserve;
driving myself in circles over this, as I did the day before.
I can't shake this; it won't stop.
Just *maybe* this isn't my love.

Then I find myself
reminiscing on the smitten times before,
so I think, maybe we can do this thing happily.
Only to return to my reality; those images stop.
Because that's no longer our love.
So, just maybe, there *is* someone else whom we both deserve.

And then comes the possibility, returning like before,
"We can work this out! Resilience is our love."
Who am I fooling? This has to stop.
How could we possibly live happily
together when I'm dishonest with myself?
This kind of love, I don't deserve.

The kind I know I deserve?
That gentle, I speak your language in love

kind;
the type I hope will never stop.
The quick to understand and listen happily
kind;
the type where I'm proud of myself
for choosing what I should've before.

I've said it before--
This is the kind for which my heart yearns; it, I deserve.
And if I'm being honest with myself,
consistently asking *this* has to stop;
I have to choose who's most important to love
if I ever want to live happily.

I had to stop and ask myself,
Is this the love I think I deserve?
And before I knew it, I left happily.

Heartbreak No More

Post a few broken hearts,
Her heart still unhardened
Instead, wisdom rests easy on her soul

Bound by this thing called hope,
She trusts her forever love,
Weaving through detours,
Just as she will meet,
At the point they're meant to be

Only difference this time 'round,
She's the prize in his eyes
So far removed,
Peering at him from the pedestal's plinth

This time 'round, poised in all her glory;
Spine erect, conscious of her value
In pursuit of his approval, an inaction cherished

"Become such as you are, having learned what that is." - Pindar

Beautiful Soul,

My hope is that my words allow you to self-reflect, look inward, and examine your union. How does it make you feel? Are you content with how things are going? Is everyone involved getting what they need from it and doing their part to strengthen the bond?

If you find yourself confirming the unfavorable, it's time to commence a new chapter--solo. Or if you think you can and will make it, ask yourself:

Is this the love I believe I deserve?

Always remember that you are worthy of gentle and patient love. Your feelings matter. And you deserve the best, nothing less.

Warmest regards,

OUR VIBE IS A REFLECTION OF OUR INNER ENERGY, SO WHEN WE’RE OFF-KILTERED, UNRESOLVED ENERGY SEEPS THROUGH. THE EFFECT OF THAT IS UP TO US.

Martika Shanel's mission is to spread the significance of self-assurance with a vision of self-love and inspiration in every heart.

about the author

MARTIKA SHANEL, Msc OSH, ARM, is a Certified Life Coach, bootstrap founder, author, speaker, and an active community member who believes in giving back.

Through her engaging and transparent speeches, she plants seeds of inspiration, instilling the importance of perseverance and seeking love from within first.

Martika is a senior safety consultant in the construction field who believes success is in everyone. As the managing member of Inspiring a Read Book Company, INSPAREAD, LLC, she works to foster enthusiasm for reading by publishing stories and messaging that resonates with the youngest of readers and beyond.

She is devoted to spreading her message and can be reached through her website and social media accounts:

www.martikashanel.com
facebook.com/authormartikashanel
twitter.com/martikashanel
instagram.com/martikashanel
tiktok.com/@martikashanel
goodreads.com/martikashanel
youtube.com/martikashanel

acknowledgements

Thanks to everyone on the Launch team who helped me so much. Special thanks to Amber, Dana, and Katie for being the best, unofficial publishing team members a girl could have; Kirsten, my amazing editor; and Kiah, the greatest cover designer I knew I needed.

Writing a book is tough and living through the experiences to produce the lessons shared is tougher. I owe the possibility of seeing the triumphs despite my odds to several people.

My Bible Camp family. Thank you for pouring into me, for giving me my first job, for ensuring I received love and care when you knew I needed it, and for the continued prayers.

To Mr. Bartley, you took me under your wing in the eighth grade and you and your wife have shed so much love my way. I'll never forget college shopping with the two of you and the consistent check-ins. Thank you for seeing my potential, for embracing me, and showing me the care I needed.

This list would be incomplete without Mrs. Davis. Since the time I was in your second-grade class, there's never been a time where you haven't shown up for me. My deepest gratitude goes to you for showing me love as a little girl at Boone Elementary School.

To the faculty and staff at Paul Laurence Dunbar and my Leaders in the Making Family. Thank you for recognizing my potential. To Mr. Duerson, my FAME award nomination for you still stands. To Mrs. Harbut who first introduced me to the importance of using transparency to spark motivation in others. To my guidance counselor and my teachers who pushed me to challenge myself.

To the faculty, my peers; Track, SGA, and Curris Center families, and friends turned family at Murray State. It's an honor to be a Racer. I appreciate you for seeing my light, embracing me for who I was, and helping to groom me into the person I am today. I once stated, 'Murray's the best thing that ever happened to me'; it rings true today. Ms. White, thank you for being the bridge to Murray and countless opportunities. And lastly, but not least, to my Doveley, Nu Rho Sorors for helping me grow as a professional, accepting me at every level, and showing up in full force to support my accomplishments to date.

Moving to the Windy City to work in commercial insurance and not knowing myself brought struggles of its own. Without Barry, my time wouldn't have been as rewarding. Thank you for showing me the ropes, being an avid supporter in all my endeavors, and for being the best manager I've ever had.

To my parents for ensuring I put education first, giving me the freedom to choose my own path, and for encouraging me to soar despite our predicament. To my dad, thank you for teaching me the importance of speaking proficiently; being independent and disciplined; and that I'm not defined by my skin color. To my late mom: you taught me grit and tenacity. Your homemade French toast with the confectionary sugar is still my favorite dish. Thank you for spreading your light, the fun times, and for never giving up. I love and miss you so much.

I'm forever indebted to my godmother, Momma Tammy. I appreciate you more than you'll ever know for everything you've done for me. You've always been here for me when I needed you--celebrating my successes since middle school, taking me school shopping and on trips, supporting all of my achievements, and holding a room for me at your home. I will, most certainly, pay it forward.

I'm eternally grateful to my family, Justina and Marla, who were prominent figures during my formative years. Thank you for taking me in as one of your babies. Ti, you taught me to stand in my truth, use my voice, and the principle of requiring respect from others. I appreciate you more than you know for stepping in as an aunt and being a positive, loving role model. Marla, you taught me to have boundaries and to fiercely be myself. Thanks so much for always thinking of me (every impromptu gift is remembered) and pouring into me. I've desperately needed you two all my life.

To more of my family: my Granny, Uncle Joe, Grandaddy Jerry, aunts Donna and Tinker, and great aunts and cousins who've shown me the most support when I've most needed it. Granny, thank you for helping me get through the darkest time in my life and being a loving and present grandmother to my babies. To my Aunt Tiny for all your love and the fun times when I lived with you. To Aunt Jeanie, Marie, Joyce, Mary, and Debbie: y'all have always shown up for me and loved me. No act of love has gone unnoticed. To my cousins James, LaQuisha, and Bryonia; thank you for being my biggest supporters, checking and loving on me. James, your willingness to always show up is forever appreciated. And to my brother; thanks for being present as a big brother. I love you.

To The Crumps: thank you for taking in a little girl from a small, country town and treating me like family. I love y'all so much. To Daddy Dale for rewarding me for my good grades. To Momma Lisa for teaching me perspective. To Crystal for being a spectacular best friend, being the light I always need, and showing unconditional love and support; and Apri and Toni for being such supportive and loving sisters. I'm thankful for each of you.

Many thanks to you, Darrell, for closure. For being the first man to greet me with a dozen roses. For being open to starting a new chapter together as father and daughter and for showing up, rain or shine, to support my author endeavors. The love and care you've shown me and my children are forever appreciated.

To Jesse. Thank you for all the great times, for being there when I needed you, for being the first person to capture my essence through a lens, and for the experience of being smitten for the first time. I will forever wish you the best and will always love you.

Amber, Adrianna, Audris, Dana, Destiny, Jennifer, Katie, Ericka, and Crystal. I could go on and on. We have rocked together through the happiest and craziest of times. Thank you for being my rock.

Much gratitude and love to those who've made the journey all the better: Gaga, Nikki Nicole, Toshanika, Mishelle, Damiko, Daysha, Chasity, Mary S., Morna, LaTarsha, Rachelle, Parlee, The Dvorjaks, Jackie, LaTasha, Cynthia, Amber D., Kiara, Jamesha, Velenzia, Jesse A., Saundria, Kelsey, Chyna, Raquan,Tara, Kat, Krystal, Shay, Lisa, Julia, Arielle, Shawna, Charity, St. Paul Family, Diamond M.,The Prices, Delainia, Elainina, Dontryse, Mylissa, and Michelle.

An extra special thanks to my Nanny. I would be here forever if I wrote all that you mean to me. You were the only constant, genuine love I had as a child. I needed your messages in college more than anything. The love you've shown is eternally with me. Smooches.

Finally, the most appreciation goes to my babies: Penelope, Hugh, and Wynn. Thank you for your warm love, teaching me how to be a better person, and for the ability to be your mom. This is the most prestigious title I could ever have, and I just hope y'all will always know how much I cherish each of you. The amount of love I have for you is immeasurable.

bonus

Try these affirmations:

I am purposeful.
I am determined.
I am courageous.
I am improving every day.
I am a light in the universe.
I am grateful for all that I have.
I am a beacon of peace and love.
I am on the path to conquering my goals.
I am in control of how I respond to others.
I am worthy of the things my heart desires.
I am healing and gaining strength each day.
I am a reflection of what I desire from others.

Made in the USA
Las Vegas, NV
05 November 2021